Are You My Fish?

by Julia Vogel
Illustrated by Matthew Williams

Content Consultant:
Gerald Brecke
Doctor of Veterinary Medicine

Are You My Pet?

visit us at www.abdopublishing.com

Published by Magic Wagon, a division of the ABDO Publishing Group, 8000 West 78th Street, Edina, Minnesota 55439. Copyright © 2009 by Abdo Consulting Group, Inc. International copyrights reserved in all countries. All rights reserved. No part of this book may be reproduced in any form without written permission from the publisher.

Looking Glass Library™ is a trademark and logo of Magic Wagon.

Printed in the United States.

Text by Julia Vogel
Illustrations by Matthew Williams
Edited by Jill Sherman
Interior layout and design by Emily Love
Cover design by Emily Love

Library of Congress Cataloging-in-Publication Data

Vogel, Julia.
  Are you my fish? / by Julia Vogel ; illustrated by Matthew Williams ; content consultant, Gerald Brecke.
    p. cm.— (Are you my pet?)
  Includes index.
  ISBN 978-1-60270-244-8
  1. Aquarium fishes—Juvenile literature. I. Williams, Matthew, 1971- ill. II. Title.
  SF457.25.V64 2009
  639.34—dc22

2008003642

Note to Parents/Guardians:
This book can help you teach your child how to be a kind, responsible pet owner. Even so, a child will not be able to handle all the responsibilities of having a pet. Since diseases can be passed from animals to humans, veterinarians suggest that adults take care of aquarium cleaning. Adults should set up tanks and electrical equipment.

Table of Contents

Is a Fish the Right Pet for Me?	4
What Kind of Fish Would Be Best?	7
Where Should My Fish Live?	12
What Else Do Fish Need?	17
What Does My Fish Eat?	20
How Do I Get to Know My Fish?	22
How Do I Stay Safe Around Pet Fish?	25
How Do I Keep My Fish Healthy?	27
Words to Know	30
Further Reading	31
On the Web	31
Index	32

Is a Fish the Right Pet for Me?

Do you like funny fish faces? Do you like watching colors, patterns, and movement? Do you want a quiet, indoor pet?

Then a fish may be the pet for you! There are many to choose from. What kind should you pick?

Pet Fact:

There are more than 28,000 different kinds of fish. Seahorses and sharks are both fish!

Guppies

What Kind of Fish Would Be Best?

Some wild fish live in freshwater streams or ponds. Other wild fish live in the salty ocean. First-time fish owners should choose freshwater fish. They are easier to care for.

Guppies are fun first fish. Male guppies come in many colors. Some have long, fancy fins. Guppies like to live together. Get more than one! Males guppies chase female guppies. You should put more females than males in your tank.

Many people start with goldfish. But they poop a lot! Goldfish tanks are hard to keep clean. They are not the best first fish.

A betta is another good first fish. A male betta can be green, blue, red, or purple. They have long, beautiful fins. Another name for betta is "Siamese fighting fish." Only one male betta should live in your tank.

Goldfish

Betta

Mollies, tetras, and barbs are all good choices. Ask a veterinarian to help you decide. Talk to your parents and friends who have fish. Visit a pet store. You need to know which fish you want before you set up your tank.

Pet Fact:

Tetras and many other fish need warm water. If you pick warm water fish, you will need a heater. Keep a thermometer in the tank. Check how warm the water is every day.

Where Should My Fish Live?

An aquarium is a glass or plastic water tank. Choosing the right size tank is important. Big tanks hold more fish, but they can cost a lot of money. Fishbowls cost less than aquariums, but do not give fish much space. To start, a good size tank for a few fish holds 10 to 20 gallons (38 to 76 L) of water.

Your tank needs other things to be a home for fish. It needs a lid to keep fish in and dust out. It needs a pump to bubble air into the water and help fish breathe. Your tank also needs a filter. A filter helps clean the tank. It catches bits of old food and waste in the water.

Water from your sink has chlorine in it. Chlorine can kill fish. Get rid of chlorine before putting your fish in the tank. Let the water adjust itself overnight or use a bottle of chlorine remover from the pet store.

Where you place your aquarium is important, too. A full water tank is heavy. Put it on a strong table or counter. Place it away from sunny windows. Too much sunshine can heat up the water. Put the tank near an outlet. You will need to plug in the pump, filter, and heater.

Pet Fact:

Fish use their gills to breathe in the water. Gills have slits that open and close when a fish breathes.

What Else Do Fish Need?

Many fish like to poke around the tank bottom. Gravel gives fish places to dig. Fish also like to hide. Add plants, rocks, or a plastic cave for hiding places.

Every fish owner needs a small net. Use it to scoop leftover food and dirt from the water. You can also use it to scoop up fish when it is time to clean the tank.

Every day, check that the pump, filter, and heater are working. Every week, change some of the dirty water for clean water.

Pet Fact:

Ask an adult to help you set up your aquarium. Everything needs to be ready before you bring your fish home.

What Does My Fish Eat?

Fish flakes have the basic food your fish needs. Always buy the right flakes for the kind of fish that you own. Give your fish as much food as it can eat in five minutes. Too much food makes the water dirty and the fish sick.

Fish also love treats. Buy healthy treats at the pet store.

How Do I Get to Know My Fish?

Fish cannot learn to come when you call, but they learn to come to the top of the water at feeding time. Get to know your fish by watching them.

Maybe one fish eats more than others. Maybe one likes to hide. The way fish act in the tank is a clue to how they act in the wild.

Pet Fact:

A tank can have more than one kind of fish. Remember to choose fish that get along, such as guppies and tetras.

How Do I Stay Safe Around Pet Fish?

Wash your hands carefully before and after touching your fish tank. Never touch the tank's electric equipment or cords. Always ask an adult to set up or fix the pump, heater, or filter.

Pet Fact:

Every few weeks, ask an adult to check the filter. Once or twice a year, put your fish in an extra tank and help an adult clean the whole aquarium.

How Do I Keep My Fish Healthy?

Watch your fish carefully. Are they eating well? Are their fins drooping? Are they swimming on their sides or acting strangely?

If one fish looks sick, set up a hospital tank. Putting the sick fish in the hospital tank protects the other fish.

Sometimes white fuzz may grow on a fish. White spots may appear on its body and fins. Call a pet store owner or a veterinarian. You may need medicine drops to put in the water.

Keeping your fish healthy and safe will let you enjoy this colorful new friend for life!

Pet Fact:

If you decide not to keep your fish any more, find it a good home. Do not put your fish in a toilet or nearby pond or stream. Most aquarium fish cannot live outdoors.

Words to Know

aquarium—a tank to hold fish or other animals.

chlorine—a chemical used to kill germs in water. It can poison fish.

filter—a machine that helps clean a tank by catching dirt floating in the water.

fins—thin skin on a fish's body that helps it move in water.

fish flakes—special food made to give fish all their basic daily nutrition.

gill—a part of a fish's body that takes oxygen from water.

thermometer—a tool used to measure temperature.

Further Reading
Macken, JoAnn Early. *Goldfish*. Milwaukee, WI: Weekly Reader Early Learning Library, 2004.
Mills, Dick. *Aquarium Fish*. New York: Dorling Kindersley, 2000.
Scott, Peter. *The Complete Aquarium*. New York: DK Publishing, 1995.
Silverstein, Alvin, Virginia Silverstein, and Laura Silverstein Nunn. *Fabulous Fish*. Brookfield, CT: Twenty-First Century Books, 2003.

On the Web
To learn more about fish, visit ABDO Publishing Company on the World Wide Web at **www.abdopublishing.com**. Web sites about fish are featured on our Book Links page. These links are routinely monitored and updated to provide the most current information available.

Index

B
barb 11
betta 8

C
chlorine 15
cleanup 12, 18, 25
colors 4, 7, 8

D
digging 17

F
filters 12, 15, 18, 25
fins 7, 8, 27, 28
fishbowl 12
food 12, 18, 20, 22, 27
freshwater 7

G
gills 15
goldfish 8
gravel 17
guppy 7, 22

H
heaters 11, 15, 18, 25
hiding 17, 22
hospital tanks 27

L
lids 12

M
maintenance 11, 18, 25
medicine 28
molly 11

N
nets 18

O
ocean 7

P
patterns 4
pet store 11, 15, 20, 28
plants 17
plastic caves 17
pumps 12, 15, 18, 25

R
rocks 17

S
seahorses 4
sharks 4
sickness 20, 27, 28
sunlight 15

T
tanks 7, 8, 11, 12, 15, 17, 18, 22, 25
tetra 11, 22
thermometers 11

V
veterinarian 11, 28

W
warm water 11
watching fish 4, 22, 27
wild fish 7, 22